Original title:
Fruitful Reflections

Copyright © 2025 Creative Arts Management OÜ
All rights reserved.

Author: Elias Montgomery
ISBN HARDBACK: 978-1-80586-291-8
ISBN PAPERBACK: 978-1-80586-763-0

Savoring the Delights

A banana slipped, oh what a fate,
Did the fruit trip, or was it fate?
Peaches giggle while they swing,
In the orchard, joy we bring.

Juicy grapes burst, a playful squeeze,
Wobbling on vines like silly bees.
Pineapple tops dance with flair,
Laughing together, without a care.

Seeds of Insight

Ponder the melon, round and wise,
With stripes that whisper, 'Surprise!'
Lemons chuckle, sour yet bright,
Making faces, what a sight!

Cherries in pairs, oh so sweet,
Their giggles make laughter complete.
Each seed a story, each bite a cheer,
Sharing secrets, bringing near.

Lush Landscapes of the Soul

In the garden where pineapples stand,
Waving their crowns, they take command.
Oranges roll with undying glee,
A citrus party, come take a spree!

Watermelons in stripes, like clowns,
Bouncing in laughter, never frowns.
In this patch, where joy plants roots,
Every fruit sings, in giggling hoots.

Rippling Waters of Wisdom

The waterfall of juice, a delicious stream,
Splashing the senses, a flavor dream.
Avocados wink, they know their worth,
Adding laughter to the mirth.

Coconuts chuckle on sandy shores,
Telling tales of the ocean's roars.
With every splash, wisdom unfolds,
In this fruity world, humor beholds.

Juices of Memory

In the blender of my mind,
Whirled thoughts collide like fruit,
Banana peels and peachy squeals,
Who knew nostalgia's so cute?

Mango mischief on a spin,
Lemon laughs can't be contained,
Sipping on the past wins,
So many smiles, unchained!

Coconut whispers tales of old,
Berry crunches add some cheer,
Zesty zest makes moments bold,
Juicy giggles, loud and clear!

Thus I blend my days away,
In a smoothie of delight,
With each sip, I laugh and play,
Memories won't lose their bite!

Garden of Contemplation

In my mind, a patch of greens,
Carrots dance and tomatoes twine,
Spinach giggles, kale preens,
Herbaceous jokes in the sunshine!

Peppers popping, what a sight,
Radishes rolling, quite the cheer,
Cauliflower dreams take flight,
In this garden, fun is near!

Squash sings notes of pure delight,
Beans juggle wisdom for the meek,
As cucumbers twirl in bright,
Life's secrets in every peak!

As I wander, laughter grows,
In rows of thoughts, odd and grand,
Each veggie shares its quirky prose,
In this grove, I happily stand!

Ripened Dreams

In the orchard where thoughts bloom,
Apples chuckle on each tree,
Peaches ponder, dispel gloom,
Even cherries burst with glee!

Dreams hang low, ripe for the pluck,
Pineapples grin with spiky flair,
Oranges roll, no room for luck,
Juicy secrets fill the air!

Underneath this fruity spree,
Watermelon winks with zest,
A fruit salad's wisdom, you see,
Comes with a side of jest!

So I gather, munch, and smile,
In this realm of whimsical fate,
Each bite's a giggle, worthwhile,
Ripened dreams can't help but celebrate!

Sweet Echoes of Yesterday

Sugary whispers float about,
Candy-coated moments sweet,
Lollipop laughs, there's no doubt,
Memories dance on sticky feet!

Brownies break the silence fast,
Cookies giggle with delight,
Every bite, a shadow cast,
Laughing flavors in the night!

Marshmallow mists swirl with grace,
Fudge fudge-faces in a row,
Jelly beans in a silly race,
Echoing, "Watch us go!"

So, I savor every laugh,
Nostalgia spreads like frosting,
In this cake of joy, I chaff,
Sweet echoes, never costing!

Nectar of the Soul

In a garden lush, where laughter grows,
Bees buzz around wearing tiny clothes.
Each sip of honey, sweet on the tongue,
Leaves us chuckling, just like when we're young.

Peaches wear blush, quite the fashion trend,
While bananas slip, making jokes never end.
Grapes gossip softly, a juicy delight,
Whispering secrets all through the night.

Whole melons dance, oh what a sight,
Juggling roundness that feels just right.
Each bite is a giggle, a fruity delight,
In this playful orchard, joy takes flight.

Vineyards of Reflection

Among the vines where we take a stroll,
Ripe berries hang, playing peek-a-boo role.
Wine glasses clink, a symphony sweet,
As we toast to grapes with wiggly feet.

Cork pops like laughter from a good joke,
Stumbling tipsy, we dance and provoke.
Barrels of stories, aged like fine cheese,
Who knew reflections could come with such ease?

Each sip is a chuckle, a giggly cheer,
Who knew grapes had such a sense of humor, dear?
With every swirl, a new tale unfolds,
In vineyards where laughter never gets old.

Chocolate-Covered Memories

In sweet little boxes, memories hide,
Wrapped up in laughter and joy, our guide.
Fruits dipped in chocolate, a treat so divine,
Who knew a berry could make us feel fine?

Strawberries blush, covered in fudge,
While cherries roll, giving sugar a nudge.
Nutty adventures within every bite,
Leave us giggling long into the night.

Truffles and bonbons, a chocolate parade,
Each one a story, an escapade made.
With every sweet taste, we savor the fun,
Chocolate-coated smiles, bright as the sun.

The Weight of the Harvest

Baskets are bulging with fruits all around,
Picking them off, there's laughter abound.
Each apple a giggle, each pear a delight,
While pumpkins roll in the autumn moonlight.

The scale tips over, oh what a mess,
"Weight Watchers won't like this," we confess.
Tomatoes keep blushing, caught in a squish,
As we weigh our troubles, let's make a wish.

Dancing through fields, oh what a strain,
Carrying produce like it's just a game.
With every ripe fruit that we joyfully heft,
The heart feels lighter, laughter's the gift.

A Symphony of Harvests

In a field where laughter grows,
The cows wear hats and strike a pose.
Chickens cluck in rhythmic beat,
While veggies dance on wobbly feet.

A pumpkin tried to sing a tune,
But rolled away beneath the moon.
The crops unite in merry cheer,
As ants conduct the band so dear.

Tomatoes giggle in the sun,
While onions join to have some fun.
A patchwork of mismatched glee,
Where nature's humor is the key.

So grab a basket, join the show,
For every fruit has got a glow.
With silly hats and tunes in mind,
Harvest joy, and laughter find!

Harvest of Thoughts

In a garden full of silly dreams,
Radishes float in dreamy streams.
A brainstorm sprouts like leafy greens,
While broccoli plots wild schemes.

Ideas bounce like bouncing beans,
As peas debate their many means.
Strawberries share some fruity laughs,
While grapes compose their witty drafts.

Corn pops up with jokes galore,
Zucchini's got a stand-up floor.
Here thoughts grow ripe, then fall like rain,
A harvest of giggles, joy, and gain.

So tend the thoughts that come to play,
And watch them bloom in a funny way.
For every idea will take root,
In the garden where laughter is the fruit!

Bounty of the Mind

A caper here, a jest over there,
My mind's a market, quite the fair!
With apples of wit and pears of cheer,
Every thought's a snack to steer.

I spied a melon with great flair,
Claiming it danced without a care.
While lemons giggle, bright and zesty,
Creating lemonade, fresh and testy.

Ideas ripe upon the vine,
Bananas slip on humor fine.
A clever punchline here and there,
Makes every moment light as air.

So gather round this quirky stall,
Where laughter's bounty fills us all.
In the garden of the bright and bold,
Each little jest's more precious than gold!

Whispers of the Orchard

In an orchard where shadows tease,
Peaches giggle upon the breeze.
With cherries chuckling side by side,
Each secret's ripe, they cannot hide.

A grapevine whispers tales quite strange,
While lemons plot a zesty change.
The apples know the silliest sights,
As laugh tracks drift through sunny nights.

A shy little fruit, the kiwi shy,
Dreams of stand-up, oh, my, oh my!
While pears tell jokes that never land,
Leaving giggles sprouting 'cross the land.

So stroll among the leafy chats,
Where fruit's as funny as the cats.
In nature's glow, with joy we cope,
As laughter weaves the threads of hope!

Reflections in Garden Paths

In the garden where I tread,
Tomatoes whisper tales of dread.
They tell of worms, who wear a tie,
Sipping tea as bugs pass by.

Carrots hiding in the ground,
Swear they've heard the funniest sound.
Radishes rolling, in fits of glee,
Joking, "Look, we're still so leafy!"

The peppers strut with vibrant flair,
Claiming they're the best in air.
While cucumbers giggle and tease,
"Bet you can't catch us with a squeeze!"

Yet in this plot, the laughter grows,
As laughter wanders where love sows.
Each plant a jester, in life's sweet show,
Their silly ways, the seeds we sow.

Vibrant Memories

Underneath the apple tree,
Squirrels share a joke or three.
The fruit is ripe, or so they say,
"Just one more bite, and I'll be gray!"

Bananas have a stick-on grin,
Always slipping, never kin.
"Peel me back for laughs galore,
But hold your breath, I might just roar!"

Berries dance in wild delight,
Claiming they're the stars tonight.
Raspberries with a cheeky pout,
"Mess with us, we'll scream and shout!"

Every memory, sweet and bright,
Is etched in humor, pure and light.
With every laugh, the past we weave,
In vibrant colors that we believe.

Whirlwind of Cultivation

In the dirt, I spin and twirl,
Seeds of laughter start to unfurl.
With every scoot, the plot expands,
While worms hold dances, hand in hands.

The herbs all gather, plotting schemes,
While mint whispers of fresh dreams.
"Basil, join us for some puns,
Zucchini's got the best of runs!"

Bees buzz by, with stories bold,
Of pansy kings and marigold.
"Pollinate this, just for kicks,
We're free to prank, we're not just licks!"

As tendrils twist and vines embrace,
There's joy and laughter in this space.
A whirlwind spins amidst the cheer,
Nature's jesters, ever near.

Petals of Wisdom

In the garden of silly blooms,
Petals gossip, sharing rooms.
"Roses are red, but daisies know,
We're here to steal the garden show!"

Sunflowers stand, heads held high,
Pointing out clouds that float on by.
"Look at that one—it's shaped like cheese!
Do you think it tastes as good as peas?"

Lilies chuckle with grace divine,
Whispering secrets through stem and vine.
"Wisdom grows on playful soil,
Each petal's laughter, and less toil!"

Gather 'round, plant friends so dear,
Let's celebrate this gardening sphere.
For laughter sows the seeds of cheer,
And wisdom blooms with every year.

The Palette of the Heart

In a world of colors bright,
Doodles dance with pure delight.
A banana slips on the art,
We giggle, oh, that's just the start!

A strawberry wears a tiny hat,
Sipping tea while a cat sits flat.
Grapes paint stories on the wall,
Every splash makes laughter sprawl!

When apples blush with a cheeky grin,
They play a tune on a violin.
Each stroke a tickle, each hue a tease,
In this gallery, we laugh with ease!

Mixed up colors, oh, what a sight,
The heart sings loud, from morning to night.
So grab a brush, let's join the fun,
In our palette of joy, we've just begun!

Honeyed Visions

A jar of honey in the air,
Bees buzzing without a care.
They dance in circles, oh so sweet,
Wobbling as they land on their feet!

Cakes are stacked and smiles abound,
Syrup rivers flowing around.
Butterflies wear tiny crowns,
As giggles float through nectar towns!

Sticky fingers, what a bother,
But who can frown, we all just smother!
In laughter's grip, we take a dive,
In honeyed dreams, we all feel alive!

So here's to sweetness, let's all cheer,
With every scoop, we hold dear.
In this land of giggles and fun,
Honeyed visions for everyone!

In the Shade of the Grove

Under trees where the apples drop,
A squirrel dances, then takes a plop.
His acorn hat goes spinning round,
While laughter echoes through the ground!

Peaches giggle, ripe and juicy,
As the sun shines, they get quite moody.
"Let's have a party," one shouts with glee,
"Bring your friends, come climb the tree!"

Mangoes swing, they've learned to fly,
While watermelons start to cry.
"Don't be sad; just join the fun!"
In the grove, we all become one!

So let's rejoice in nature's plea,
Where laughter floats as wild and free.
In the shade, we find our groove,
Together, we dance, laugh, and move!

The Dreamer's Garden

In a garden where dreams sprout wide,
Tomatoes wear a coat of pride.
Dancing carrots, what a sight,
Twirl around in morning light!

Onions giggle, trying to hide,
With laughter bubbling just inside.
They shed tears, but don't you fret,
In this garden, there's no regret!

Spinach chats with mint so fresh,
While peas gather to discuss their mesh.
"Let's grow a party," says basil with flair,
In this dreamland, there's magic in the air!

So come and join this silly crew,
Where every sprout has something new.
In the dreamer's garden, fun's the theme,
And every moment's sweeter than it seems!

The Aroma of Possibility

In the garden of dreams where ideas sprout,
Lemonade thoughts make the frowns twist about.
Bananas are slipping on laughter so bright,
Peaches in pajamas dance under the light.

Pineapples prance with a crown on their head,
Carrots in costumes bring joy when they're fed.
Berries burst forth with giggles and cheer,
Creating a feast that draws everyone near.

Oranges giggle in sun-kissed delight,
While grapefruits giggle and roll out of sight.
The bonkers brigade of the fruit salad crew,
Brings jokes and puns to the fruitful brew.

So let's pick a grape or two, just for fun,
As laughter and fruit combine, oh what a run!
With a slice of zest, life's a grand buffet,
Where every sweet moment leads laughter your way.

Blossom of Intentions

A daisy wishes on a tart cherry pie,
While lemons exchange stories with keys to the sky.
Plums plot adventures of wiggly worms,
As apples debate all the fruity terms.

Kiwi insists that it's king of the day,
While coconuts giggle and dance all the way.
Raspberries wearing their fanciest clothes,
Make puns about love, oh where it all goes!

Tomatoes get saucy with silly old jokes,
As bok choy joins in, much to the folks' pokes.
Lettuce wraps laughter, and sprouts stand up tall,
In this garden of giggles, there's room for us all.

With petals so soft and intentions so sweet,
We tread on good vibes with mirth in our feet.
So let's bloom some joy in this colorful place,
And savor the smiles on each fruit-covered face.

The Orchard Within

In the orchard of dreams, fruits swing on a vine,
Nuts cracking wise jokes, feeling simply divine.
Peach trees are gossiping, branches all sway,
While cherries are plotting a comedic display.

A pear makes a pun about fruit that's gone bad,
While coconuts laugh, saying, "Aren't we just rad?"
Fig trees serenade the squirrels up high,
While avocados sing out a green lullaby.

Grapes have a gala, with clusters galore,
Making jam out of laughter that's hard to ignore.
Every fruit's a character in this vibrant play,
Where the humor is ripe, ensuring our stay.

So grab that old basket and fill it with cheer,
Dance through the orchard, let joy reappear.
Each bite is a giggle, a crunch of delight,
In this merry old orchard, we'll laugh through the night!

Nectar of the Heart

In the garden of giggles, the nectar is sweet,
With hearts made of jelly, there's no better treat.
Honeydew dreams float like bees in the air,
While oranges waltz without a single care.

Strawberries whisper their secrets of zest,
Pineapples pine for a fruit-lover's fest.
Watermelons burst forth with a bubbly delight,
Tickling our senses like stars in the night.

The nectar of laughter, it drips from the leaves,
Where every fruit sprinkles joy, none ever grieves.
With a wink and a nudge, each berry joins in,
Creating a chorus where laughter won't thin.

So take a big splash in this whimsical stream,
Where every fruit moment is sweeter than cream.
With hearts full of nectar, let's savor the art,
Of ridiculous joy, the nectar of the heart.

Roots Beneath the Surface

In the garden, weeds hold hands,
Carrots chatting, making plans.
Potatoes giggle, hiding their eyes,
While onions plot beneath blue skies.

Beneath the dirt, a rumbling crew,
With roots that sway and dance anew.
Radishes wear their glowing hues,
While squash sends out its cheerful snooze.

The worms all wink as they dig deep,
Racing through the soil in a laugh-filled sweep.
Compost chats about its funky smell,
As tiny sprouts wish each other well.

So if you see the veggies beam,
Know they're caught up in a leafy dream.
With roots entwined in playful jest,
Beneath our feet, they love their quest.

The Color of Solitude

In the orchard, apples roll and hide,
Moping near the cider side.
"Why so glum?" a peach inquires,
"Join our dance, it never tires!"

The plums just shake and tease the pears,
"Come on, fruit, don't stay in layers!"
But oranges, bright, just start to pout,
Saying, "Let's get juiced — no doubt!"

Bananas slip with laughter bright,
Screaming, "We're peelin' with delight!"
A grape rolls by, so snug and small,
"Why not join us? It's a ball!"

Yet solitude has its quirky flair,
A sour lemon clings to air.
But in this fruit salad of the free,
Even loneliness can be a spree.

Petals and Paradoxes

Daisies grumble in a sunny row,
"Why are we always just put on show?"
Tulips boast, "We're red with pride,
While violets just sip from the side."

Busy bees buzz with infinite schemes,
"Who will make honey from all our dreams?"
But roses sigh, with thorns in tow,
"How come we're always put on a show?"

Wind whispers secrets through the leaves,
While petals fall, and the garden grieves.
But sunflowers smile in their tall embrace,
"Life's a joke in this flowery place!"

With colors bright and scents that tease,
They dance through summer's warm, sweet breeze.
Paradoxes of bloom and woe,
Here's laughter found in petals that flow.

Tending to Inner Landscapes

In a pot of soil, a seed starts to dream,
Thinking about life and prancing in steam.
Water sings softly, nourishing grace,
While raindrops giggle, splashes to face.

Thoughts grow wild, like weeds in the air,
Each one a flower with quirks to spare.
Roots dig deep, embracing the muck,
Whispers of life in a botanical chuck.

A cactus frets in its prickly way,
"Why can't I join the fray today?"
While ferns unfurl with a fanciful shake,
"Loosen up, friend, for goodness' sake!"

Inner landscapes flooded with cheer,
Fungi cracking jokes ear to ear.
Tending to minds where laughter flows,
In this garden, anything goes!

Sweet Surrender to the Silence

In quiet moments, I munch on pears,
Hoping no one notices my messy cares.
Bananas whisper secrets of the night,
While apples giggle, green and bright.

I ponder life with a juicy bite,
As oranges roll with laughter in sight.
Pineapples crown me—just so divine,
And cherries blush at the sips of wine.

Grapes are gossiping, oh what a scene,
While papayas share tales from between.
Each fruit has a story, juicy and clear,
I smile at the fruit bowl, oh dear, oh dear!

So here's to the silence, a comical friend,
Where laughter and fruits never seem to end.
I toss a peach, and it lands in style,
A sweet surrender, oh what a smile!

The Ethereal Orchard

In the orchard of dreams, where fruits jest and play,
Nuts start a band, but the apples just sway.
Peaches wear hats, strawberries dance round,
While oranges juggle, pure joy to be found!

A kiwi told jokes that tickled the air,
Bananas rolled laughing, without a care.
Avocados in shades, a hipster delight,
Filled with the laughter of silly fruit fights.

Ripe melons gossip under the sun,
Promising giggles, oh what fun!
Cherries run races, all pitted and bold,
In this orchard of laughter, stories unfold.

So let's join the fruits in their vibrant spree,
Where joy is abundant, wild, and free.
With every soft bite, we giggle and cheer,
An ethereal orchard, we hold so dear!

Ripe with Intuition

Beneath the bright leaves, a mango does twirl,
While lemons make plans to give life a whirl.
A fig with a wink offers up its delight,
While strawberries chuckle through day and night.

Intuition is ripe, like a pumpkin in fall,
While avocados whisper, "Let's have a ball!"
With plums as the band, oh what a craze,
While pears hold the spotlight in funky displays.

Cherries are cheeky, dressed up all fine,
Inviting the fruit crew to sip on some wine.
Pineapple's wisdom, a slice of the truth,
Gives me a chuckle, reviving lost youth.

So let's toast to life, in this fruity affair,
With laughter and sweetness beyond compare.
In the realm of the ripe, our hearts they shall sway,
With intuition so fresh, we laugh all day!

The Symphony of Growth

In gardens where tomatoes bloom bright,
A squirrel steals one, what a sight!
He dances away with glee in his step,
While I ponder my own veggie prep.

The carrots wiggle, they're ticklish too,
The beetroot blushes, isn't it blue?
Each sprout has a story, a giggle to tell,
As I chase off the crows, oh what the hell!

The sunshine laughs, the clouds roll on,
The peas are singing their silly song.
With every harvest, a joke or two,
Laughter sprouts with the veggie crew.

In this garden, chaos reigns supreme,
With buttered corn, what a tasty dream!
I plant my hopes, I sow them deep,
Waiting for Chuckles, in harvest we reap.

The Color of Contemplation

I ponder peaches, fuzzy and round,
They giggle softly, 'Come chase us down.'
With every bite, a juice parade,
Sticky fingers, oh what games we've played!

The melons whisper, 'We're full of fun!'
Water fights beneath the summer sun.
They dribble down chins, a slip-n-slide,
In this fragrant mess, we all confide.

Bananas teasing with their yellow hue,
'Peel us, peel us!' they chant anew.
Slipping and sliding, it's a fruit ballet,
Contemplating laughter, our sunny buffet.

The grapes conspire, small clusters of cheer,
Each bubble of laughter bubbles near.
In colorful chaos, sweet jokes take flight,
Fruits of laughter, oh what a delight!

A Cornucopia of Memories

Thanksgiving came, what a crazy feast,\nWith cranberry sauce run away, at least!
The turkey danced, took a bow so grand,
While I grabbed the last slice with shaking hand.

Pumpkin pies stacked like a wobbly tower,
I dare not blink, I feel the power.
Each bite a memory, each laugh a tale,
As cousins race for the last big kale.

The veggies giggle, in colors so bright,
They leap from the table, a comical sight.
With laughter intertwined, we reminisce clear,
A cornucopia of joy to revere.

And when dinner's done, we strike up a band,
With spoons as our drums, we'll all take a stand.
In the blend of all flavors, our hearts take flight,
A memory banquet, oh what a night!

The Abundance of Now

In the orchard, apples dangle low,
With whispers of sweetness, a subtle glow.
They giggle as they sway in the breeze,
Join me, they say, for a snack if you please!

Oranges are bouncing, as bright as the sun,
Slip on their peels? Oh, that would be fun!
Their citrusy laughter fills the air,
While I juggle fruits without a care.

The grapes roll around like they're on parade,
Taking a tumble, but never afraid.
With each little burst, they're tickled pink,
A toast to the moments, it's time to drink!

So here's to the now, let's cherish and shout,
With laughter as fruit, let worries devout.
In the garden of giggles, let joy be the guide,
For the abundance of life is best shared with pride!

Sweetness of Solitude

In the garden where I lounge,
Bananas hang like yellow crowns.
A pear once joked about its shelf,
But now it's pondering by itself.

The grapes all giggle in a bunch,
While cherries make a daring lunch.
An apple told a peach, 'Don't pout!'
For in this quiet, we can sprout.

The lemons laugh, their zesty tone,
While coconuts just chill alone.
They said, 'No need for crowding here,'
'Just us, the fruits, and some good cheer!'

So raise a glass of juice, don't fret,
Alone is sweet, with no regret.
For solitude has quite a knack,
To turn the fruitcake into snack!

The Essence of Reflection

An orange sat, looking so wise,
Said, 'I could peel away the lies.'
A lemon quipped, 'That sounds so sour,'
'But let's embrace this citrus hour!'

Peaches pondered, soft and round,
'In every slice, a truth is found.'
The berries chimed, in vibrant hues,
'We celebrate our quirky views!'

'Let's pop some seeds of laughter,' said,
A watermelon, green and red.
With every smile and fruity quote,
We'll sail our boat on joy, afloat!

So here's to thinking, fresh and bold,
With fun reflections to unfold.
For in our sweetness, we can see,
Life's juicy moments, wild and free!

Orchard of Possibilities

In an orchard where the laughter grows,
A kiwi wore a tiny nose.
A pineapple took to wearing shades,
While avocado played charades.

The plums all danced with merry flair,
Convinced the nectarines were rare.
A fig declared, 'I've got a plan!'
To start a band, called 'The Fruit Jam.'

The cherries joined, with voices sweet,
And joined the dance upon their feet.
A tangerine took up the beat,
Together they made quite the treat!

So let's unite in this delight,
In this orchard, all feels right.
For every fruit holds dreams galore,
With every giggle, we can soar!

Ripeness in Stillness

In the quiet glow of waning light,
A banana contemplated flight.
An elder plum said, 'Stay and chill,
For ripe reflections give a thrill!'

The figs agreed, 'We've got the time,
Let's squeeze the juice of our prime.'
The avocados nod with glee,
Finding stillness is the key.

A coconut cracked a thoughtful jest,
'To rest is truly quite the best.'
The grapefruits spun in endless grace,
Creating joy in this slow pace.

So gather 'round this mellow scene,
Where laughter reigns, and life's serene.
Even in stillness, fun's revealed,
When fruits connect, their fate is sealed!

The Taste of Reminiscence

Once I ate a peach so sweet,
I heard my childhood's laugh repeat.
It rolled away and bumped my knee,
Now it's a quirky memory.

Those cherries in a tree so high,
I claimed a prize beneath the sky.
But when I grabbed with all my might,
I fell and crunched the fruit—what a sight!

A berry burst right in my hand,
It flew away, like a rubber band.
I chased it down, with giggles loud,
As berries formed a bouncing crowd.

So let us munch on memories,
Where laughter bounces in the breeze.
With every bite, a chuckle sips,
Recalling all those juicy trips.

Orchard of the Mind

In my mind grows apples wide,
They giggle as they twist and glide.
A fruit salad of thoughts runs free,
With bananas that dance in glee.

Pears wear glasses—oh what a sight!
They argue about how to take flight.
While grapes huddle, sharing their dreams,
Of juicy adventures and playful schemes.

A tangerine tells jokes so bright,
It makes the lemons laugh with delight.
But when a melon rolls too fast,
It trips the cherries, a slippery blast!

In this orchard, fun blooms like flowers,
Each thought, a fruit with joyful powers.
So swing by soon and take a bite,
Of playful memories wrapped in light.

A Palette of Ripeness

Splash of colors, fruits galore,
A canvas life we can explore.
From honeyed figs to zestful lime,
Each flavor tells a tale in rhyme.

The lemons got into a spat,
Squeezed out some juice, then took a nap.
While mangoes hid, playing peek-a-boo,
With oranges chuckling, 'What's wrong with you?'

Avocados sit with a cool, green style,
Claiming the lounge chair, with a smile.
But when ragged bananas start to dance,
They all join in for a silly prance!

This palette paints a sunny cheer,
With laughter sprinkled, bright and clear.
So let's create and savor some fun,
With fruits of joy under the sun.

The Sweetness of Silence

Amidst the quiet, fruits conspire,
Crisp apples whisper, none retire.
A melon hums a gentle tune,
As plums sit pondering the moon.

In silent laughter, berries plot,
To sneak a nibble from the pot.
A kiwi winks with mischief in sight,
As they nibble away into the night.

With every crunch, the silence sings,
A harmony among sweet things.
Beneath the stars, they reminisce,
Of flavorful tales not to miss.

So in the stillness, take a pause,
And savor fruits—give them applause!
For in their sweetness, funny quirks grow,
Turning silence into a vibrant show.

Reflections Like Ripe Pears

In the garden of thoughts, I pluck my ideas,
Like ripe pears dangling, they tease my fears.
A bite of humor, juicy and bold,
Each laugh spills sweet, stories unfold.

With a grin like a slice, I share my delight,
Turnip-shaped worries disappear from sight.
Quips drop like apples while I dance in the breeze,
As sunshine chuckles from the top of the trees.

My mind's a fruit basket, colorful and bright,
Banana peels slipping, oh, what a sight!
Lemon zest laughter, the zest of the day,
In this orchard of giggles, I'll surely stay.

As I savor each moment, like marmalade spread,
Life's a pie fresh out, with humor as bread.
So join in my banquet of silly and sweet,
We'll toast to the wit that feels just like a treat!

The Abundance of Being

A bunch of bananas with laughter in tow,
They swing from the branch, putting on a show.
Mirth bubbles up like soda in cheer,
As we juggle our lives, and humanity, dear.

An orange a day keeps the frowns at bay,
Especially when it rolls like a merry old play.
With each juicy segment, I peel back the skin,
Revealing the giggles that dwindle within.

In this orchard of whims, under skies so blue,
I stumble on sprigs of the light-hearted crew.
We ripe up our jests, a full-hearted cheer,
With laughter like nectar, we sip without fear.

So let's dance through this grove, where the banter is sweet,
And a cherry on top makes the day feel complete.
Together we'll whirl, let our spirits break free,
In the bounteous garden of joyful esprit!

Tender Roots of Thought

Like carrots underground, my thoughts dig deep,
With wiggles and giggles, they're not hard to keep.
Sprouts of reflection bloom, what fun it would be,
To share with good friends, as hearty as peas.

In the patch of my mind, radishes play,
They wiggle around, sprouting puns every day.
With soil rich in chuckles, we harvest the cheer,
Roots run so tender, and the laughter draws near.

So let's plow through the humor, sow seeds of mirth,
In this whimsical field overflowing with worth.
As laughter takes flight on the wings of a bird,
We cultivate joy, that magical word.

With each playful till, we uproot heavy thoughts,
Replanting bright dreams in the warm sunny spots.
Together we'll flourish, side by side, old chums,
With roots that grow deeper as merriment hums!

The Plentiful Mindscape

In a garden of chuckles, my brain does expand,
A cupcake of whimsy, all sweet and unplanned.
Fruits of my thinking hang ripe on the vine,
With giggles like grapes, so deliciously fine.

A hammock of humor swings softly in place,
While pineapples grin with a tropical grace.
Ideas jump forth like bunnies at play,
Each thought a green apple, chasing cares away.

In this plentiful mindscape, let's frolic and roam,
With peaches and laughter, we're never alone.
So gather 'round friends, let the joy resonate,
In this fruit-salad world, every bite is first-rate!

With each whiff of whimsy, let our spirits take flight,
Navigating through punchlines and smiles, so bright.
So come pluck a laughter, it's ripe on the tree,
In this orchard of wit, we're forever carefree!

Mindful Harvest

In a garden of thoughts, I dig deep,
Finding ideas, that make me leap.
I pluck a few giggles, a chuckle or two,
Giggling at wisdom, who knew it grew?

With each little berry, I savor the taste,
Of life's silly moments, there's no time to waste.
Some jokes may be rotten, but laughter's the key,
A harvest of humor, come share it with me!

So gather your quirks in a basket, my friend,
The fun in our lives is the best way to blend.
As we munch on our quirks, let's keep it a treat,
Mindful of laughter, it's truly a feast!

Join me in gleaning, no fruit's left behind,
With each little chuckle, our hearts intertwined.
A patch full of joy, let's sow and cultivate,
In this yield of smiles, let's celebrate fate!

Tasting the Sunshine

I woke up one day with a craving for rays,
To sample the daylight, in so many ways.
I gathered my spoon, and I scooped out some fun,
With a sprinkle of giggles, oh what a run!

The sun drips like honey, so sweet on my tongue,
It dances like fruit when a new song is sung.
Each bite of bright laughter is simply divine,
With sunshine so zesty, there's no need for wine!

I squeezed every moment, I savored each grin,
The flavors of joy, oh where to begin?
With a dash of absurdity, I feast on the day,
Tasting the sunshine, I'll laugh all the way!

And when clouds drift in, with a frown on their face,
I whip up my humor, it's the perfect embrace.
For laughter's a harvest, it never goes stale,
In the orchard of smiles, we shall always prevail!

Colors of Reflection

In a palette of life, I mix up my hues,
With splashes of giggles, and whimsical views.
Each color a moment, oh what a delight,
Painting the canvas from morning to night.

The orange of mischief, the blue of a blunder,
A sprinkle of pink for the laughs that we thunder.
With shades of confusion, all twisted and bright,
We'll frame our tomorrows, and dance in the light!

The green of old jokes, still fresh on the vine,
A rainbow of memories, oh how they shine!
I dip my brush deeply in puddles of cheer,
Creating a masterpiece, year after year.

So let's swirl our colors, let laughter take flight,
With each playful stroke, making everything bright.
In this gallery of giggles, we'll find our perfection,
Painting our world with the colors of reflection!

The Orchard of Experience

In the orchard of tales, I wander with glee,
Picking snippets of life, just waiting for me.
I shake the old branches, and watch what might fall,
A bounty of stories, I'm ready to haul.

The apples of laughter, so crisp and so sweet,
Each bite brings a chuckle, a joyful repeat.
The peaches of wisdom, all fuzzy and new,
Remind me to savor, like a soft morning dew.

A handful of oranges, for zest in my tale,
Each one holds a lesson, like setting a sail.
I gather them closely, these fruits of the mind,
With each quirk and twist, new treasures I find.

So let's toast to our harvest, of quirky delights,
In the orchard of life, we'll dance through the nights.
With laughter as nectar, come share in this spree,
In this grove of experience, let's always be free!

A Basketful of Thoughts

In a basket logs my mind,
With apples of thoughts intertwined.
Bananas slip through the cracks,
While oranges launch silly attacks.

Pears giggle on the tree limb,
Just waiting for my next whim.
Cherries wink with mischief bright,
As grapes roll in a playful fight.

Melons chime in with a tease,
Saying life's a game, if you please.
Raspberries joke, 'Don't take a bite,'
Your teeth may retreat in sheer fright!

So, gather your fruit, friend of cheer,
There's humor aplenty, oh dear!
From juicy jests to zestful glee,
In this basket, fun's the key!

The Fruit of Silence

In the orchard, quiet reigns,
A peach whispers during the rains.
The plum, feeling a tad shy,
Winks and gives a fruity sigh.

Strawberries hide in crimson hues,
While avocados tell the blues.
The banana, dressed in a grin,
Says, 'Let the silliness begin!'

An apple soaring high in thought,
Raves about the lessons it's taught.
'Silence can be a funny space,
Where fruit has its own kind of grace.'

So savor the fruits of a quiet day,
Let laughter bloom in a silly way.
For in the stillness, joy is found,
Even in silence, laughs abound!

Shadows in the Vineyard

In the vineyard, shadows play,
As grapes gossip about the day.
Wine barrels chuckle with delight,
As corks pop in eager flight.

The sun tips its hat with charm,
While figs find mischief on the farm.
Peaches roll down with a cheer,
Saying, 'Let's drink a little beer!'

Every shadow holds a scare,
Like a melon with messy hair.
Bottles sing a fruity tune,
Underneath the glowing moon.

So toast to shadows, let's be bold,
In this vineyard, magic unfolds.
With every sip, let laughter blend,
As grapes and jokes around us bend!

Nectar and Nostalgia

Sweet nectar drips with a grin,
As memories swirl, where do I begin?
The taste of summer in a jar,
Brings back tales from afar.

Lemons squint as they recall,
The time they took a summer fall.
Peaches laugh and hum a song,
Saying, 'We were right all along!'

Nostalgia packs a punchy zest,
With cherries wearing fancy dress.
The grapevine giggles in delight,
Recounting tales from day to night.

So sip the nectar, savor the cheer,
Let memories dance, bring the fun near.
In every flavor, a story hides,
Where laughter and sweetness always collide!

The Orchard of Unspoken Words

In the orchard, quiet and sly,
Apples chuckle, as peaches sigh.
Banter blooms on branches high,
Grapes gossip as they pass by.

Pears pratfall, they trip and roll,
Plums perform an acrobatic stroll.
Cherries giggle, they can't control,
While citrus fruits just play the role.

In shadows where the nectar drips,
Ripe berries share their fruity quips.
Bananas slip on their own scripts,
While kiwi dreams of friendship trips.

So next time you wander through,
Listen close; they'll share a clue.
In this grove, the laughter's true,
For fruits will speak, if given you.

Seeds of Contemplation

In a garden where thoughts donate,
Seeds sprout with a jolly fate.
One thinks deeply, while others wait,
Pineapples joke about their plate.

Melons ponder the weather's tease,
As fig trees dance in playful breeze.
Cucumbers marvel at how to please,
And beans debate the best of cheese.

The pumpkins roll with laughter loud,
Chasing thoughts, feeling quite proud.
Sunflowers nod, forming a crowd,
As radishes grow beneath the shroud.

Each seed a thought, each fruit a jest,
They muse about life—it's all a test.
While nature giggles, doing its best,
Together they laugh, a happy fest.

Ripened Moments

In a basket, moments gather round,
Ripe memories are waiting to be found.
A banana slips, the laughter abound,
While grapes burst forth with a joyful sound.

Peaches wink with a cheeky grace,
As cherries roll, they quicken their pace.
Lemon zest, with a smirk on its face,
Banter beams in this fruity space.

Each slice reveals a tale so fine,
Like jellybeans dancing on a line.
Fruitful capers in sunshine divine,
Bringing chuckles, all in good time.

Moments carouse in juicy delight,
Blushing berries twinkle at night.
Together, they spin tales in flight,
As laughter ripens under starlight.

Sunlight Through Leafy Veils

Through leafy veils, sunlight peeks,
While oranges whisper, sharing freaks.
Bananas yawn, taking humble seeks,
And strawberries gossip about their peaks.

In dappled light, the apples sway,
Witty puns at the end of the day.
Tomatoes blush, still have much to say,
Eggplants chuckle in a purple ballet.

Secret tales in shadows unfold,
With every fruit, a legend told.
Limes cackle about being bold,
As berries giggle, chasing the gold.

Sunlight plays in a merry dance,
Fruits unite in a playful chance.
Together they sing, a joyous romance,
In this vibrant, wild expanse.

The Abundant Mosaic

In a garden so bright and wide,
Tomatoes in sunglasses, full of pride.
Carrots in boots, on a dance floor,
Kicking up dirt, always wanting more.

Lettuce twirling, a waltz in the breeze,
While radishes laugh, dropping to their knees.
Fruits in a bowl organize a band,
Making a jam, not just by hand.

Bananas swing low, so easy to peel,
Pineapples wearing crowns with zeal.
With each giggle, a berry will sway,
In the mosaic of colors, they play.

So sip on your juice, and let out a cheer,
For the laughter of veggies is fabulous here.
In this quirky patch, take a stroll and bask,
Under sunshine's warmth, it's a whimsical task.

Essence of the Seasons

Springtime giggles, a fruit parade,
Apples in hats, and oranges serenade.
Berries on scooters zooming around,
In a playful riot, not making a sound.

Summer arrives, like a juicy surprise,
Watermelons sunbathing under blue skies.
Cherries in flip-flops, doing a jig,
Peaches in sunlight, becoming quite big.

Autumn rolls in, with a crunch and a cheer,
Pumpkins in bowties, everyone here.
Grapes in a line, like children at play,
Hoping that winter won't take them away.

Winter comes knocking, but look, what a sight!
Citrus in scarves, oh what a delight!
Bananas in boots, slipping with glee,
In this seasonal dance, let's all join the spree!

Prosperity in Silence

In the quiet kitchen, a feel of delight,
A pickle whispers secrets in the night.
Avocados, avocado, what tales will you share?
Guacamole dreams float into thin air.

The fridge is a treasure, it holds all the cheer,
Kiwis in tuxedos clink glasses of beer.
The grapes form a council, with wisdom to spare,
In a silent debate, no one else is there.

Zucchinis ponder their future so bright,
While onions ponder if crying's polite.
A fruit bowl convenes, intentions so grand,
Hoping to end up on toasted bread planned.

So here's to the whispers of flavor and fun,
In the still of the kitchen, the laughter's not done.
In this quiet prosperity, so silly and round,
Each bite is a moment of joy to be found.

The Tapestry of Abundance

Weaving together, the fruits and the greens,
A tapestry formed from whimsical dreams.
Bananas and berries share stories of old,
While cauliflowers chuckle, both brave and bold.

Pineapples gossip about life on the tree,
While grapes compete in a race for the 'free'.
Melons roll over, giggling all night,
In this patchwork of laughter, everything feels right.

Plums dressed in feathers, ready to prance,
Kohlrabi in clogs, prepared for the dance.
With each little stitch, a joke to unfold,
In this colorful fabric, the tales are retold.

So sip your sweet smoothie, rejoice with a laugh,
For the tapestry grows as we take our own path.
In every bright bite, there's a giggle, a cheer,
In this bountiful weaving, fun is always near.

Thoughts Like Grapes

My mind's a bunch, all tangled tight,
With thoughts that bounce, like grapes in flight.
Some sweet like honey, some sour too,
They roll and giggle, just like I do.

In shadows cast by vines so green,
I ponder why my socks don't glean.
A fruitless search for socks that twirl,
As grapes just laugh and form a whirl.

With every squish, a new idea,
Like juice that drips, I'm full of cheer.
I pick my thoughts, a basket wide,
As chuckles burst, they cannot hide.

When life gets heavy, I take a snack,
A grape of joy, no need to rack.
Revealing laughter, ripe and bold,
My thoughts like grapes, a story told.

Melody of Abundance

In orchards bright where laughter flows,
A tune is born that tickles toes.
The apples sway, in breezes dance,
A symphony of fruit, a big romance.

Bananas croon, in yellow hue,
While blueberries whisper, 'Hey, we're cool too!'
The cherries chirp, oh what a sound,
This boppy jamboree, unreal, profound.

Each bite a note, a juicy rhyme,
I hum along, it's snack o'clock time.
With every crunch, a giggle's made,
In this fruit party, no need for trade.

Melodies of laughter, sing along,
In this vast orchard, we all belong.
With every nibble, joy received,
A fruity tune, simply believed.

The Tapestry of Life's Harvest

A quilt of colors, fruits all sewn,
In stitches bright, they've surely grown.
With every berry, and orange peel,
Life's funny fabric, oh what a reel!

Pineapples wear their crowns with pride,
While fruit flies crash the retro ride.
The peaches blush, oh what a sight,
In this wacky loom, all feels just right.

Kiwi threads, green and fuzzy,
Weaving giggles, never fuzzy.
A tapestry where laughter blends,
Each fiber laughs, as friendship mends.

With every stitch, a joyous lore,
In nature's quilt, who could ask for more?
A harvest bright, of chuckles wide,
In this tapestry, we all abide.

Reflections Beneath the Canopy

Under leafy roofs, I take a peek,
With sunlight flickering, laughter speaks.
The lemons grinned, so tangy bright,
While coconuts giggled, oh what a sight!

Shadows dance where humor thrives,
Each fruit tells tales of silly lives.
The avocado winks, smooth and sly,
As mangoes wink back, oh my, oh my!

In this comedy of peeking fruits,
I find myself, in silly suits.
Reflections ripple, like laughter's flow,
Under the canopy, the joy will grow.

Beneath this shade, the world's delight,
Is fruit's funny nature, a carefree flight.
In dappled light, my thoughts take wing,
Under this canopy, we laugh and sing.

The Garden of Whispers

In the garden, gossips bloom,
Tomatoes laugh while peas consume.
Carrots gossip in the dirt,
While radishes wear grass for a skirt.

A cabbage rolled away from foe,
While onions cried with tears aglow.
The daisies dance with bees so sly,
As pumpkins ponder, 'Why am I shy?'

The herbs are bold, with secrets spry,
Thyme's got jokes, oh my, oh my!
Chives chuckle, with roots so deep,
As nature keeps her quirks to keep.

So visit this plot, where giggles thrive,
Each seed's a joke, that's how they survive!
In a realm where veggies speak,
The laughter's ripe, and growing sleek.

Reflections in a Citrus Bowl

A lemon sat, with quite the sass,
It asked an orange for some class.
'You roll through life, oh what a zest,'
While limes just sighed, 'We're all so blessed.'

The grapefruit grinned, with rosy pride,
And joked about how sweet they hide.
They ponder life, in juicy throes,
While peeling back their quirky woes.

Pineapples wear crowns, feeling grand,
While grapefruits scheme a citrus band.
They sing of sunshine in a bowl,
With laughter bubbling, fresh and whole.

So take a sip of this fruity cheer,
These jokes are ripe, let's all draw near!
In citrus worlds where chuckles swell,
Each fruit's a story, and all's quite well.

Blossom and Shadow

In bloom, old petals take their stand,
While shadows stretch, as bright as planned.
The blossoms tease the leaves above,
'You're such a shade, but we still love!'

A rose rolled by, great pink delight,
While daisies jived in morning light.
Lavender giggled, all in bloom,
'Who needs a vase? We smell the room!'

In whispers soft, the berries sang,
As butterflies flew, their colors dang.
The sunflowers swayed, heads high and proud,
While night came softly, like a cloud.

With laughter held beneath the night,
The blossoms blush, shy from the light.
In shadows cast by moon's embrace,
Nature's humor paints the place.

Pears in the Twilight

Two pears sat low, with thoughts profound,
They pondered life, and spun around.
'What's the point of hanging here?'
While crickets tuned their tunes so clear.

One pear jested, 'Let's take a leap!'
But the other said, 'I'd rather sleep!'
They shared their dreams of juicy fame,
'If only folks could know our name!'

The wind agreed, with whispers sweet,
While squirrels gathered for a treat.
'Let's start a band,' the pears declared,
A jam session, it's all prepared!

The twilight wrapped them in its glow,
With laughter rippling, soft and slow.
In the orchard's heart, they found their way,
A pair of pals, who love to play.

Seeds of the Self

In the garden of my mind, I sow,
Dancing thoughts like seeds in tow.
They sprout with laughter, some take flight,
While others sit, and simply bite.

Digging deep for joy each day,
Comparing ideas like kids at play.
Some are gnarled, others quite round,
Yet all are treasures waiting to be found.

Planting dreams in rows so neat,
Watering them with rhymes so sweet.
A patch of giggles, a twist of fate,
Who knew introspection could be this great?

With every chuckle, a sprout will rise,
Reflecting back in giggly disguise.
So here I stand, with a grin so wide,
In this garden of self, I take pride.

Radiant Harvest

In fields of thought, I roam and roam,
Gathering silliness, feeling at home.
Each fruit I find, a jest to share,
With juice of laughter, floating in air.

Sunshine smiles and tickling breeze,
Whispering secrets among the trees.
I pluck the puns and let them grow,
Sprinkling wit like it's confetti flow.

The harvest dances, ripe and bright,
Each bite a chuckle, pure delight.
Bananas slip, and berries tease,
In this patch of mirth, I'm at ease.

So pile the fruits in a big ol' sack,
Silly apple pies when I get back.
With my comical feast, I take my stand,
In the orchard of jest, where joy is grand.

Blossoms of Clarity

Petals of thought, so many blooms,
Like quirky socks in crowded rooms.
Each idea opens, bright and loud,
Shouting 'hello' to the waiting crowd.

Through tangled vines of amusing chat,
I pluck the quirks, you know, like that.
The colors burst in giggles so pure,
In this garden, there's always more.

The bees buzz by, with tales to spill,
Gathering nectar that gives us a thrill.
And as they dance from bloom to bloom,
I giggle along, chasing the gloom.

With every flower, a chuckle grows,
In this world of whims, anything goes.
So let's all plant, and water with cheer,
In our garden of laughter, year after year.

The Fruit of Reflection

In my mind's orchard, a jester's delight,
The fruit hangs low, oh what a sight!
Each pear a pun, each peach a jest,
Reflecting smiles, it's truly the best.

Coconuts clunk with a humorous thud,
While grapes giggle in a juicy flood.
I gather the laughter, one by one,
In this crazy garden, we all have fun.

From citrus rounds to apples of mirth,
Each bite reveals the joy of worth.
So munch on wisdom with a grin so bright,
Each taste a memory, a silly sight.

Let's toast to the laughter that we create,
In this fruitful reflection, it's never too late.
So hold up your glass and take a big sip,
For each giggle harvested is a sweet trip.

Reflections in Autumn's Glow

The apples hang low, quite a sight,
With squirrels plotting their autumn bite.
Leaves dance like crazy, all aglow,
While pumpkins ponder, 'Are we in a show?'

Cider flows freely, so do the grins,
As friends swap tales of their harvest wins.
A pie by the window, aroma divine,
But watch out for crumbs that you'll surely find!

The acorns fall down with a thud,
The trees whisper secrets, all wet with mud.
Gather 'round, laugh, don't take it too slow,
In this autumn dance, let your worries go!

We toast to the harvest, with giggles and cheer,
In the season of change, we hold our loved ones near.
May this glow of the fall keep our hearts in tow,
As we savor these moments, just watch the show!

Juicy Revelations

A peach told a pear, 'I'm feeling quite fine,'
The berries chimed in, 'You should see our vine!'
Melons rolled over, laughing so sweet,
While citrus got zesty, dancing on their feet.

The talk of the garden, oh what a fuss,
Each fruit sharing tales, creating a buzz.
'What's ripe and what's rotten?' they laughed 'til they cried,
In this fruity gossip, no one could hide!

Watermelon's giggles sent seeds in a spin,
While cherries just formed a bright red grin.
Bananas slipped up, lost track of their peel,
In this wacky fruit talk, every joke is a steal!

So here's to the harvest, the laughter we sow,
In juicy revelations, let your laughter flow.
With each taste of friendship, the world feels right,
Lemonade dreams, oh, what a delight!

The Splendor of Moments

In the orchard we gathered, what a fine crew,
Chasing after apples, oh, what a view!
Lemonade splashes, like laughter in the air,
With every small moment, joy is laid bare.

The sun paints the sky, a vibrant affair,
While berries blush softly, stripping down bare.
The tales of the grapevine are silly and bright,
As peaches play tag with the sparkling light.

An orange jested, 'I'm zestier than thee!'
While bananas just slipped off to take a spree.
Amidst all the chaos of sweet juicy fun,
Each moment a treasure, each laugh gently spun.

So let's raise a glass to this fruit-filled day,
To the splendor of moments that never decay.
For in every shared giggle, we grow and we thrive,
In the orchard of laughter, we're truly alive!

The Palette of Fruitful Days

A canvas of colors, so bright on display,
Bananas in yellow, strawberries in sway.
Apples are blushing with cheeks full of pride,
A splash of the berry, oh, it's a wild ride!

Crafting a smoothie, a masterpiece blend,
With splatters and giggles, we call it a trend.
Grabbing a scoop from the cheerful buffet,
The palette of flavors turns mundane to yay!

Mangoes and kiwis, dance in the bowl,
As laughter erupts, it's a flavor patrol.
Whipped cream like clouds, on top in a swirl,
In this fruity gallery, we'll let laughter unfurl!

So here's to the fruit, and days sprinkled bright,
With splashes of joy, our spirits take flight.
In every sweet moment, let our colors play,
In the palette of life, let's seize the day!

Harvested Dreams

In the basket of my mind, laughs abound,
Tree of wonders, plump and round.
Each idea like berries, ripe and sweet,
Giggles echo with every bite we meet.

Chasing squirrels in the autumn breeze,
Wearing hats made of leaves, if you please!
From acorns to grapes in our playful scheme,
Harvesting joy, oh, what a dream!

Fruits of ponderings, sticky and bright,
Banana peels slide with comedic delight.
Oranges juggling on my thought's parade,
Laughter erupts, this moment won't fade.

Let's toast with punch made of whimsy and cheer,
An orchard of humor, come gather near!
In this field of chuckles, we sway and twirl,
Harvested dreams, let's give them a whirl!

Echoes of Orchard Days

In orchard days filled with silly sights,
Apples giggle, caught in their flights.
Pirouetting pears, dancing with glee,
Nature's talent show, come see, come see!

Ripe peaches wearing shades in the sun,
Claiming they're royalty, oh what fun!
Grapes rolling down, a slippery trail,
Chasing after each other without fail.

Cider spills tales of mischief and cheer,
As we toast to the laughter gathered here.
With each burst of flavor, smiles unite,
Echoes of laughter shining so bright.

Memories blend like a fruit punch mix,
Days of delight filled with silly tricks.
In this orchard, we dance and sway,
Echoes of joy that forever will stay.

Beneath the Canopy of Thought

Beneath the leaves, ideas pop and crack,
Coconuts chuckle, plotting their snack.
Clouds gather fruit that rain down in fun,
While visions of laughter outweigh the sun.

Silly squirrels spin tales with flair,
Finding ripe rhymes hidden everywhere.
In this leafy refuge, giggles abound,
As antics of acorns roll round and round.

Mangoes whisper secrets in a buzz,
While wisdom comes dressed with a playful fuzz.
We bounce on ideas like bouncing balls,
Beneath the canopy, laughter enthralls.

So grab a thought, its juice is divine,
With a dash of humor, it's sure to shine.
Beneath the branches, we'll happily throng,
Harvesting chuckles, all day long!

Juices of Memory

In a blender of time, flavors collide,
Memories swirl in a jester's glide.
Bananas and berries join the parade,
Creating a cocktail of laughter and shade.

Oh, the zesty tales of a citrus feast,
Tangy and ticklish, to say the least.
Each sip a reminder of things gone by,
With a twist of lime, we laugh and sigh.

Watermelon whispers of summer's glee,
As we frolic through juice like fish in the sea.
Straws like unicorn horns in a merry dance,
Together we blend in a playful trance.

So let's raise a glass filled with bright, silly schemes,
To the juicy concoctions of our wild dreams.
The cups overflow with fun and delight,
Sipping the past, everything feels right!

www.ingramcontent.com/pod-product-compliance
Lightning Source LLC
Chambersburg PA
CBHW060136230426
43661CB00003B/449